THE POLICE HIST

POLICE HISTORY MONOGRAPH NUMBER 1

━━

NOTES FOR FAMILY HISTORIANS

━━

ISSN 0951-8800

ISBN 0 9512538 0 8

Les Waters

Superintendent, Cambridgeshire Constabulary.
Secretary of The Police History Society.

First Published by The Police History Society 1987

ISBN 0 9512538 0 8

All rights reserved. No part of this publication may be reproduced or transmitted in any form or by any means, electronic, mechanical, photocopying, recording or otherwise without the prior permission of the publisher.

Printed by Cambridge City Council, The Guildhall, Cambridge.

CONTENTS

Foreword	1
Introduction	2
The Local Nature of Policing	2
A Short History Of The Police	3
Pre 1829 The Parochial System and the "Old Police"	3
1829 The Dawn Of The "New Police"	5
1833 Lighting And Watching Police	5
1836 The New Borough Police	6
1839 The First County Police Act Etc	6
1842 An Attempt To Prop Up The Parochial System	7
1856 Universal County Police At Last	7
1856 To Date Consolidation And Development	8
Documentation And Records	8
a) What Records Were Kept	8
b) Survival Of Records	10
c) Research And Examination Of Records	12
Other Background Material	13
a) Published Material	13
b) The Police Gazette	13
c) The Police And Constabulary Almanac	13
d) Other Police Periodicals	13
Special Constables	14
Non Home Office Police	14
Note For The Future	14
Notes	16

Appendix A
Current U.K. Police Forces And Their Addresses   18

Appendix B
County Police Forces - Dates Of Formation   22

Appendix C
List Of Known Police Museums   23

Appendix D
Police And Constabulary Almanac   24

Appendix E
Notes On "Police" Periodicals   31

Appendix F
Notes On The First Report Of The Constabulary
Commissioners   38

Appendix G
Metropolitan Police Records Of Service
Public Record Office Information Leaflet No 53   43

Selected Bibliography   46

Illustrations

Inside front cover;

Cambridge Borough Police, group photograph, all officers named, 1865.
(Cambridge Police Museum)

Inside rear cover;

One of the more interesting advertisements from a 'Police' periodical from "Police And Fire" 1st June 1880 for "The Official Tricycle".

A regular 19th Century advertisement from "The Police and Constabulary Almanac" for "Cording and Co's Waterproof Police Capes" 1877.

Police History Society, Notes For Family Historians

FOREWORD

The Police History Society was formed in 1985 and expanded rapidly during 1986. As the Society became better known so it received publicity from many local and family history periodicals. This publicity led to many enquiries from family historians who found that they had an ancestor who had been a parish constable or a police officer. Many such family historians found that they were unable to obtain information to help with their research and as Secretary of the Society I began to receive a steady trickle of letters seeking pointers to new sources and avenues of enquiry.

In January 1987 I took a bundle of unanswered correspondence of this type to the Police Staff College as a form of light relief from a staff course and these notes sprang from the type of questions which the writers had posed. The charming assistance of Daphne Ruddiman and her staff in the Police College Library also encouraged the research which went into the following pages.

I am delighted that the Chairman and Committee of the Police History Society saw sufficient merit in the notes to wish to use them in what I earnestly hope will be the first of a series of many Police History Monographs. I am grateful also for help and advice from Bob Bartlett, Maureen Scollan, Paul Williams and Mr. C.G.A. Parker of Hazell and Co.

Crown Copyright material in Public Record Office Information Sheet 53 is reproduced by permission of the Controller of Her Majesty's Stationery Office.

It only remains for me to freely acknowledge any errors in these notes as my own responsibility and not that of the Police History Society. It is to be hoped that these notes will run to future editions and with this in mind I would welcome any criticism or constructive suggestions for improvement or expansion.

Les Waters
Cambridgeshire Constabulary
Divisional Police Headquarters
Parkside
Cambridge.

May 1987.

THE POLICE HISTORY SOCIETY

NOTES ON POLICE HISTORY FOR FAMILY HISTORIANS

INTRODUCTION

These notes have been prepared as an introductory guide for family historians who find that they have family connections with the Police Service in England or Wales and require information on their police ancestor. The notes concentrate upon three main areas;

1. General background information on police history,
2. Primary and secondary historical source material,
3. Survival of historical material and how to find and use what remains.

THE LOCAL NATURE OF POLICING

Policing in England and Wales has always been essentially a local function and even today there is not a National Police Force. This has important consequences for the family historian.

a. There is no central repository for police personnel records (or other police records or archives).

b. There is no standard practice in the way in which local police forces have established and maintained historical archives.

c. It is essential to know where a person served as a police officer if there is any hope of finding any further information. The correct current Police Force must then be established for the location before enquiries can be made.

d. There has, over the years, been a steady move towards fewer and larger police forces. There are now only 43 forces (Home Office forces) in England and Wales. As smaller forces have amalgamated or been swallowed up so records have been lost or destroyed.

Appendix A shows current police forces and lists their Headquarters.

More detailed information on current forces can be obtained from "The Police & Constabulary Almanac" published annually by R. Hazell & Co, P.O. Box 39, Henley-on-Thames, Oxon, RG9 5UA. This book is available in good reference libraries or from the publishers and contains an excellent current gazetteer. Appendix D also deals with the Almanac as a source document.

Police History Society, Notes For Family Historians

A SHORT HISTORY OF THE POLICE

Whilst some form of policing can be traced back to Saxon and Norman periods it is important to realise that organised policing as we know it in the form of the "new police" dates back only to 1829 and the formation of the Metropolitan Police. (1)

It is not the intention to give here a detailed history of policing. This is comprehensively covered elsewhere and the reader is referred in the first instance to the "History of Policing in England and Wales" by T.A.Critchley, and for greater detail to the "History of the English Criminal Law" by Sir Leon Radzinowicz. The subject cannot be ignored completely however and the following is put forward as a list of significant dates and phases in the development of policing in England and Wales to give some practical assistance to the family or local historian.

Pre 1829 - The Parochial System and "The Old Police"

As set out above it is possible to trace a form of policing back to pre Conquest times. The Anglo Saxon idea of "Frankpledge" was a joining together of the community with all its members bound by social obligation to keep the peace. From this developed the idea of the Tythingman and the Hundred Man being responsible for ensuring that the system worked. The system was stiffened by the Normans whose Sheriffs were required to hold special courts known as the "view of frankpledge" at which the Tythingmen presented to the court details of crimes committed and other matters and were required to produce wrongdoers. If that was not possible fines would be levied against the whole community. Eventually the post of Tythingman became that of the Parish Constable. By the 13th Century this post had emerged as an unpaid office served in turn by members of the community. The post holder still had to make presentments to the Manorial Court or Court Leet but also had powers and responsibilities to keep the peace and to pursue wrong doers with the raising of "hue and cry". No uniform went with the post but a staff of office was usually passed to each person who served in his turn. (2) The Parish Constable was to some extent a subordinate officer to the Justice of the Peace under whose direction he would have normally worked.

The post of Parish Constable was not popular. It was unpaid and took the holder away from his normal work. In some places the responsibilities of the post were onerous. Failure or refusal to serve was punishable by fine. Some paid the fine to avoid the post but in many places the practice of appointment of a paid deputy was more attractive. By the 16th Century such practice was common, often the same substitute serving for some years. The cheapest substitutes were those who could, through age or infirmity, find no other work and it is not difficult to see how the post of Constable often fell into disrepute.

In the towns the Constable was responsible for setting the watch. Watchmen also originally served on a rota basis, keeping watch by night for felons and strangers. Eventually in some incorporated boroughs it became the practice for the Corporation to pay the Watch. In some places powers to do this came from 18th or 19th Century local Improvement Acts which variously included paving, lighting and watching powers.

In the Metropolis in addition to the Watch and the appointment of Parish Constables there were some advances in policing made during the 18th Century. Mainly these advances centred on Bow Street. There the Fielding Brothers held their courts. (3) They were honest magistrates in a profession where many 'trading justices' made their fortune from the mis-application of the criminal law. The Fieldings introduced a new force, a small number of paid constables, known as the "Bow Street Runners", who could be directed by the Magistrates to go anywhere in the country to investigate reported crime. Also the Fieldings introduced printed circulars on crime and wanted persons, which were distributed throughout the country as a precursor to the Police Gazette. (4) In addition some successful experiments were made with uniformed mounted patrols to deter highwaymen. The model of a handful of loyal plain clothed officers attached to a police office serviced and controlled by a small number of magistrates was taken up in the Middlesex Justices Act 1792 which created seven additional magistrates offices in London. (5)

The family historian who can number a Bow Street Runner among his ancestors is a rare and lucky person. However virtually no records appear to have survived from this fascinating period of police history. The Bow Street Police Office itself was sacked during the Gordon Riots and all the records were burnt. Something of the flavour of the work of these interesting characters can be gleaned from Percy Fitzgerald's "Chronicles Of Bow Street Police Office" (1888) and Henry Goddard's "Memoirs Of A Bow Street Runner" (1956).

Another development in London at the end of the 18th Century was the introduction in 1798 of a Marine Police. This service owed a great deal to the ideas of Patrick Colquhoun, one of the Middlesex Justices. Initially the service was funded by the West Indian merchants to prevent thefts. In 1800 however the organisation was put under the Thames Police Office, a further example of the Bow Street model under the 1792 Act.

During the early years of the 19th Century various experimental mounted, unmounted, day and night patrols operated at different times from Bow Street while the politicians wrestled with the problems of reconciling English freedom and the need to control crime and public order by effective policing.

Other police related organisations which emerged in the 18th Century were the many local "Associations for the Prosecution of Felons". There were hundreds of these in existance in different locations. They were essentially local associations of householders or landowners who paid a subscription to a fund which was used to assist any members who became the victims of crime. The association would usually advertise a reward following an offence committed against a member and would also pay the fees of a Bow Street Runner or a thieftaker together with prosecution expences in certain cases. Associations also sometimes actually employed "policemen" to patrol the streets. Some Associations were general in their application while others were specifically formed to deal with certain types of crime, such as poaching or horse stealing. Detailed

records of many of these Associations survive in County Record Offices
The records often include membership lists as well as details of crimes
committed against members. Many Associations continued in existance
until the second half of the 19th Century and a handful, now dining
clubs, still exist. (6)

Another feature of this period was the professional thieftaker who
carried out a very specific role in tracing and arresting offenders
either for a fee or for a reward, upon conviction, paid by the
Government, the loser or a local association. Little has been written
about thieftakers generally although a great deal has been written about
some of the most infamous of the breed such as Johnathan Wilde, the self
styled 'Thieftaker General'. (7) There are no specific records relating
to thieftakers but an occasional mention of individuals can sometimes be
found in contemporary newspaper reports of crime or trials in the 18th
and early 19th Centuries.

1829 - The Dawn Of "The New Police"

After many previous attempts to modernise the largely inadequate
policing arrangements of the London area, the Metropolitan Police was
formed by Sir Robert Peel. The Metropolitan Police Act became law on
19th July 1829 and the first two Commissioners were Sir Charles Rowan
and Richard Mayne. These two tireless individuals built up the force
from nothing to a large and well organised body in a matter of mere
months. (8) The more senior officers of the Force, Superintendents,
Inspectors and Sergeants, were in the main appointed from persons with
experience as N.C.O.s or Warrant Officers in the army and navy. For most
of the 19th Century the bulk of the Constables recruited to the
Metropolitan Police originated from outside London, many in fact being
agricultural labourers. A fascinating account of the way in which the
Metropolitan Police was first organised can be found in the early
chapters of David Ascoli's "The Queens Peace".

1833 - Lighting And Watching Police

In this year the Municipal Corporations Commissioners toured the country
examining the state of affairs of local government in the incorporated
boroughs. One subject examined was the state of policing in each
borough. The evidence given before the Commissioners was often reported
verbatim in local newspapers and this, together with the Commissioners'
Reports, can shed some light on the state of policing or watching in
these 178 boroughs. Although the first modern police date from 1829
there were more rudimentary police forces in many towns prior to that
date and the ubiquitous Parish Constable was to be found everywhere.(see
above)

In 1833 there was a legislative change which had far reaching effects on
local policing. The Lighting and Watching Act of that year could be
adopted locally by a certain number of property owners following a
simple procedure of calling a properly constituted meeting for the
purpose and appointing Inspectors from their number. They were then

empowered to levy a rate and, among other things, to appoint policemen. This Act was adopted in a great many places, usually where the system of Parochial Constables was failing to meet the needs of the community. As the Act only provided for local inhabitants to pay for their own policing there must generally have been some problem in existence which residents were prepared to pay to solve.

Some County Record Offices do have on deposit the accounts and minute books of Lighting And Watching Act Inspectors. [9] Occasionally appeal papers can be found in Quarter Sessions papers where individual residents have appealed against the requirement to pay a Lighting and Watching Act rate. In some instances these items relating to rating appeals may be the only remaining indication of the existance of a Lighting And Watching Act force. If minute books or accounts survive they usually contain details of all the ratepayers attending meetings and paying rates. Minute books can also be a rich source of material with detailed accounts of appointments, indiscretions, achievements and general activities of the appointed full time and temporary supernumary officers. Occasionally a real gem will survive in the form of the day book of some little force which will literally contain a daily blow by blow account of policing in the often barely literate words of the officers of the day. [10] A classic recent book on the work of one such Force at Horncastle in Lincolnshire is "Lawless and Immoral" by B.J.Davey. A family historian who had an ancestor in a Lighting and Watching Act Force might strike lucky and find some very valuable material lies hidden in the local CRO indexed under 'Lighting' or 'Watching'. These lighting and watching forces usually existed at the parish or small town level and many only employed one or two policemen.

1836 - The New Borough Police

In this year the incorporated boroughs [11] were reorganised under the Municipal Corporations Act of 1835 which followed the report of the Royal Commission. Policing was a function of the new Corporations and new Borough Police Forces were established under the supervision of Watch Committees. Many of these forces were very small and a great deal of day to day control over forces was exercised by the Watch Committees. This level of control is usually reflected in the level of detail in the Watch Committee minutes which often contain the names of individual officers.

1839 - The First County Police Act Etc

In this year the report was published of the so called " Constabulary Commissioners". This Royal Commission had been appointed in 1836 to review the policing needs of rural areas. One of the three Commissioners was Sir Charles Rowan, by then a very experienced Commissioner of the Metropolitan Police. The second Commissioner was the reformer Edwin Chadwick. Both were very keen to see a rural constabulary following the Metropolitan Police model and the report paints a graphic picture of lawlessness in a country which was simply not equipped to deal in any meaningful way with crime in the majority of areas. The Report is

strongly recommended to the historian who wants to get detailed
background material on the state of law and order at the time although
given the views of two of the three Commissioners some of the
illustrations in the report may be less typical than the report
suggests. The original submissions made to the Commissioners are in fact
available amongst the Home Office papers in the Public Record Office at
Kew [12] and these contain more detailed local information from around
the country. Appendix F gives further notes on this important report.

In 1839 the first County Police Act found its way onto the statute book.
The act was permissive and could be adopted where the Justices in
Quarter Session decided that they should levy a rate and set up a Police
Force in a County or part of a County. The Act was rushed through
Parliament in the face of considerable apprehension concerning public
disorder involving the Chartist movement. [13]

Some Counties readily adopted the provisions of this Act immediately
while others adopted it in the ensuing years. [14] Appendix B contains a
list of the dates when the Act was adopted in different Counties. County
Record Offices and Local Studies Libraries often contain detailed
contemporary pamphlets on the relevant cases either for or against the
adoption of this Act. Where they survive these can be very useful in
indicating the policing measures in existance at the time and their
relative effectiveness and cost.

It is from this period that most of the county police forces date. Many
recruits among the senior officers came from the Metropolitan Police or
from some of the more efficient borough forces. Constables were
generally recruited locally from the labouring classes.

1842 - An Attempt To Prop Up The Parochial System

By this time the 1839 Act was clearly not going to be voluntarily
adopted by some counties. The Parish Constables Act of 1842 was an
attempt to prop up the parochial system by making available a mechanism
whereby Constables and Superintending Constables could be appointed to
serve in a paid capacity and lock-ups could be built without the
necessity of setting up a proper police force. This Act was adopted in
some places where the 1839 Act had not found favour. Records of
appointments, dismissals and disciplinary matters are generally to be
found in the Quarter Sessions Minutes in County Record Offices.

1856 - Universal County Police At Last

The County and Borough Police Act of this year finally made it
compulsory for all counties in England and Wales to establish proper
police forces. The Act followed the recommendations of the Select
Committee On Police of 1853. [15] This report again provides a detailed
insight into policing of the period and the report includes the evidence
taken from many senior officers of the day.

Those counties which had not set up county forces under the 1839 Act are shown in Appendix B. The 1856 Act also made it compulsory for some of the smaller borough forces to amalgamate with county forces. The Act also allowed for part central funding for police forces which achieved an acceptable standard of efficiency. To improve efficiency and effectiveness the Act created the posts of Her Majesty's Inspectors of Constabulary (H.M.I.s) who were required to certify annually that a police force was sufficiently efficient to attract grant.

From 1856 To Date - Consolidation And Development

During this period there has been a move towards fewer and larger police forces. The Local Government Act of 1888 set up Standing Joint Committees of County Councillors and Magistrates who took over the police committee function of the Quarter Sessions. This Act also abolished police forces in towns with a population under 10,000, reducing the number of forces in 1889 from 231 to 183. Despite continued pressure from the Home Office, the next massive wave of amalgamations did not take place until after the Second World War in the wake of the Police Act of 1946. Further strides in this direction were made in the years following the 1964 Police Act and the 1972 Local Government Act.

The period also marks the entire development of many aspects of policing as we know them today. This embraces the establishment of various specialist departments and functions, the employment of women, mechanisation, improved communications, the use of information technology and much more. All of this is well documented in Critchley's work. (16)

DOCUMENTATION AND RECORDS

a) What Records Were Kept.

Today, in common with many other areas of public service, the police service sees itself as being dominated by paperwork. In the days before the emergence of the New Police there would have been very little paperwork associated with the Parish Constable or the Watch. Even less has survived. The sort of material which did exist would have been as follows:-

> 1. **Parish Constables Disbursements.** These were often only scraps of paper listing those tasks tackled by the Constable for which some form of financial compensation was sought from the Justices. Disbursements do contain the name of the constable concerned and surviving documents do provide fascinating "snapshots" of the work of the parish constable.
>
> 2. **Parish Constables Lists.** These were the lists of Parish Constables appointed each year and were often recorded in the 19th Century in Quarter Sessions Minutes.

3. **Case Papers.** Occasionally details of depositions, complaints and court records bear the names of police officers.

4. **Minute Books.** Full details of Borough Watches and pre 1836 Borough Police can usually be found in Corporation Minute Books where these have survived. After 1836 these were generally kept as seperate Watch Committee Minutes for the incorporated boroughs. Borough treasurers accounts can also give information about police functions and costs and these often also contain the names of officers in receipt of pay or expences..

Other records routinely kept by the emerging "New Police" would have included;

1. **Personnel Books** under various titles. These gave details of all appointees, their descriptions and backgrounds and subsequent careers.

2. **Discipline Books.** Such books were usually, but not always, separate from personnel books and showed all the disciplinary matters arising. Entries in these books in the 19th Century were legion. This was no doubt caused by harsh discipline and low standards of performance by officers. [17]

3. **Occurrence Books** (sometimes known as incident books or station diaries). These were kept at police stations and recorded the day to day happenings which came to the notice of the police and the daily duties and activities of police staff.

4. **Charge Books.** These were the records kept at all stations which recorded arrests, arresting officers, charges and the disposal of prisoners.

5. **Minute Books Etc.** In addition there would have been both Minute Books and Accounts of the police committee. For the Boroughs this would have been the Watch Committee and for the County Forces it would have been the Magistrates sitting in Quarter Sessions or, after 1888, the Standing Joint Committee. For the Quarter Sessions it is worth examining not only the Quarter Session Minute Books but also the bundles of miscellaneous surviving papers from each session. [18] These papers can contain gems such as Chief Constables quarterly reports, manpower deployment lists, pay sheets as well as miscellaneous bits and pieces recorded by serving officers.

By the latter part of the 19th Century many more documents were being routinely kept and are still in use in one form or another to date. These would include officers' pocket notebooks, crime reports and registers, crime files, court result registers, correspondence books, lost and found property registers, registers of convicts on licence and a host of other items. In the service today it is not unusual to find a force with a list of several hundred different forms, books and registers in current use.

Other useful series of reports produced over the years include Chief Constables Annual Reports and Her Majesties Inspectors of Constabulary Annual Reports. These do not generally mention officers by name except perhaps the most senior officers, but they do provide interesting contemporary background material.

Chief Constables Annual Reports must now be produced under a statutory duty embodied in the 1964 Police Act but series of these reports dating back well into the 19th Century can be found from some forces. The sort of material likely to be found in these reports would be;
- criminal statistics
- details of non indictable offences prosecuted
- licencing matters
- police strength, recruitment and deployment
- major events and crimes during the year
- lost, stolen and found property
- fire brigade and ambulance reports where these tasks were undertaken by police.
- extraneous matters undertaken by police

Annual reports of Her (His) Majesty's Inspectors of Constabulary in the 19th Century supply information on;
- Area covered, in acres
- Population
- Acres per Constable
- Police/population ratio
- Rank structure, strength and pay scales

There are also paragraphs for each force on duties undertaken, state of stations, cells and equipment, licencing matters, level of crime, major incidents and general level of efficiency. As an example, in the 1860s, it would be normal to find a general summary of comments each year from the Inspector for each District followed by between one half and one page of information on each force.

19th Century newspapers also provide useful material. Watch Committee meetings are often subject of verbatim reports and even crime seems to have been reported in a fairly comprehensive and believable fashion.

One other neglected source of information is the group photograph. Many police museums have a selection of group photographs of police officers, often of the whole force, generally taken between the 1880s and 1930s. Often these photographs contain the names of all those who are featured. An excellent early example from Cambridge Borough Police is reproduced herein.

b) Survival Of Records.

This is the real problem for the historian. Generally speaking police records have only survived in a fragmentary and piecemeal fashion. It is worth exploring the reasons for this in a little detail. Most modern police forces date from pre 1860 and their first buildings date from this era. Generally speaking most of these original buildings have long since been either demolished or have ceased to be police buildings as forces have grown or simply updated their accommodation. As buildings were vacated it was usually the task of some administration officer to see that the new building was not cluttered with the accumulated junk of ages and old records have been systematically destroyed as their potential future value was not appreciated. Similarly most police forces have been subject to one or more amalgamations and these again proved to be occasions when the old was deliberately swept away as organisations tried to establish new identities. In addition the paper pulping demands of two world wars also took their toll and reduced still further the chance survivals.

Confidentiality has always been a necessary part of police work and so this has become a part of the 'police culture' This has also contributed to the problem as, over the years, police officers have been reluctant to hand over their records for preservation by other agencies. Only the Metropolitan Police are covered by the provisions of the Public Records Act 1958.

Until very recently, the police service generally had never really valued its history and even today there is no national police museum although a growing number of individual forces do now have some form of local collection. (Appendix C lists the known current police museums). Instead of police forces having a rational archiving policy for their records for the benefit of future historians, most have "destruction policies" geared to clearing the decks of unwanted paper to maximise the operational use of buildings and staff. There is currently considerable pressure on Chief Constables to continually improve effectiveness and efficiency and this climate is not conducive to devoting scarce resources to establish police archives.

The net effect of all this is that it may be safest in the first instance to assume that a record has not survived.

Some records do however have a slightly higher chance of survival than others. Old personnel and discipline books have often survived as they have always been seen to be highly confidential and valuable. Often these records were kept in the same books for decades and so a whole book might have been kept when other records were destroyed, not just because of its intrinsic value but because at the back of the book were records which were reasonably current.

Other records with a higher chance of survival were those which were not actually in the hands of the police, such as Quarter Sessions Minutes and Watch Committee Minutes and Accounts. These have often found their way to County Record Offices or other well known local collections and museums.

With the above exceptions other survivals are of almost a chance nature. Indeed some survivals have come about because of the curiosity of individual officers who on occasions have saved some book from destruction to keep it and return it to a Force Museum many years later. On other occasions in the distant past old records have no doubt been "borrowed" by collectors never to be seen again.

c) Research And Examination Of Records.

This is a difficult problem with no simple answer. Some forces have deposited their records with County Record Offices or local museums. Other forces do have some sort of museum or archive of their own. The Metropolitan Police have some of their own records and have deposited others in the Public Record Office. Generally speaking most forces do not have any sort of resident professional archivist or any research facilities. Many forces do have one or more officers who are interested in maintaining a small museum or historical collection but they are operational staff who do work relating to police history in their own time. Reproduced at Appendix C is the result of a survey, undertaken by Elizabeth Lally, a professional Museum Curator with West Mercia Police, which shows those forces which do have some sort of Police Museum.

Given the hotch potch of different facilities in different Forces it is obvious that in the majority of cases it would not be realistic to expect answers to detailed questions from family historians as the necessary research would be very time consuming.

Where no professionally staffed police museum exists one useful line of approach might be to write to the Force Administration Officer, at the force headquarters address, with a general query to establish whether or not personnel books or discipline books survive for the place and period concerned and then to ask if it is possible for the material to be examined at the headquarters of the force or put on temporary deposit at the local County Record Office. By offering to search the material yourself you will of course reduce the burden on police staff, but this approach would only be worthwhile with material which is at least 70 to 100 years old or issues of confidentiality may come into play. This might bring forth the desired response but remember that there is no statutory duty imposed upon the police to undertake historical research or make this sort of material available and your enquiry is only one non urgent matter in front of an officer with insufficient time and resources to get on with practical policing problems. From the experiences of some historians it appears that some police forces simply do not answer correspondence of this nature.

In the Metropolitan Police area material of genealogical value is held at the Public Record Office, D.2 and F.4 Branches of the Metropolitan Police, The Commissioner's Reference Library and the Metropolitan Police Historical Museum. The P.R.O. publish a useful leaflet on Metropolitan Police Records held there under Ref MEPOL (P.R.O. Information Leaflet No 53). This leaflet is reproduced at Appendix G by permission of the Controller of Her Majesty's Stationery Office.

If details of an ancestor in the Metropolitan Police are required it is suggested that an initial enquiry be directed to the Metropolitan Police Museums co-ordinator, Mr P. Williams, c/o Room 1334, New Scotland Yard, Broadway, London SW1H 0BG. Mr Williams will then be able to give guidance on what material may be found where. Again enquiries of this nature cannot be given a high priority and a delayed response should be expected.

OTHER BACKGROUND MATERIAL

a) Published Material

When researching material relating to the police in a particular place at a particular time there are a number of other sources worth considering. There are published histories of most police forces in the United Kingdom. These vary enormously in quality as do the many police autobiographies which have been published. A useful bibliography on "Police in England and Wales, 1829 - 1979", has been published by the Police Staff College and is available, free of charge, from the Librarian at The Police Staff College, Bramshill House, near Hartley Wintney, Hampshire.

b) The Police Gazette

The Police Gazette is an official periodical with restricted circulation which has been in print since the mid 18th Century under a variety of different names. It contains details of important crime, absentees and deserters from the armed forces, arrested persons thought to have committed crime elsewhere and other matters. Insertions in the Gazette carry the names of head officers of police as well as the names of victims and criminals. The Police History Society is currently working on a project to re-publish 18th and 19th Century surviving copies of the Gazette on microfiche. This important new source containing millions of names should become more generally available in libraries during 1987.

c) The Police And Constabulary Almanac

The Police Almanac is a very important and virtually unknown source of information from 1858 to date. Details of this serial are contained in Appendix D.

d) Other Police Periodicals

The Police Review magazine has been in print since January 1893 and is a news and information magazine for police officers. It contains a great deal of interesting material concerning police officers and their work and conditions of service. The Review is indexed annually and biographical material on senior police officers or police celebrities does regularly appear indexed under name and Force.

There are a number of other "Police" periodicals of one sort or another which have appeared over the years. A summary of those items produced before 1920 which appear in the British Library is contained in Appendix E. Many items which appear from their titles to be central to the study of police history are in fact of little or no value and Appendix E may be useful in saving time researching inappropriate material.

SPECIAL CONSTABLES

In addition to the developments outlined above there was, and indeed still is, a different type of police officer, the Special Constable. Today the Special Constabulary is known as the Police Reserve. Its officers are part time unpaid volunteers and they are of tremendous assistance to the regular force. The first statute which empowered Justices to swear in citizens as Special Constables in the event of a special emergency dated from 1662. This power of appointment was used in some areas on a fairly regular basis and some fairly organised groups of special constables did play an important part in law enforcement in some areas of London. Generally however large numbers of Special Constables would only have been sworn in during some major emergency. Other statutes in 1820 and 1831 [19] enabled Magistrates to swear in Special Constables as a preventative measure and to compel persons to serve in the office. Special Constables were used extensively during the Reform Bill Riots and Chartist Disturbances.

Provision was made in the Municipal Corporations Act of 1835 for the appointment of a number of Special Constables each year in October to be called upon during the year to support the regular force on a warrant declaring that the regular force was unable to maintain law and order.

Occasionally records can be found in County Record Offices listing those sworn as special constables but other than that very little has survived. Even in more modern times virtually no records seem to have survived within police forces to indicate the tremendous personal contribution to law and order made by many Special Constables during the General Strike and the two World Wars.

NON HOME OFFICE POLICE

All the above discussion relates to what are now termed "Home Office Police Forces", that is the normal police of England and Wales. Reference to an ancestor being a Constable could also apply to some other non Home Office Police, the most common of these being Railway Police. Constables were employed by railway companies from the 1830s and were needed not just to prevent trespass and safeguard the company's property but also to try to minimise the worst excesses of behaviour of the navvies constructing the railway. Other non Home Office Police related to various docks, harbours, markets, parks, canals and more latterly to the Atomic Energy Authority and various airports. Generally speaking any records relating to these police would need to be traced in the same way as other documents relating to those undertakings. [20] Some material on these forces can be found in the Police Almanac as outlined in Appendix D.

NOTE FOR THE FUTURE

The Police History Society may be able to connect some enquirers with possible sources of assistance via its quarterly Newsletter if suitable

Society members volunteer to assist. Material for the Newsletter should be sent to;

The Secretary,
The Police History Society,
Superintendent L.A. Waters,
Cambridgeshire Constabulary,
Divisional Headquarters,
Parkside,
Cambridge.

Any contributions, by family historians, to add to this paper would be most appreciated and could be incorporated in future versions

NOTES

1. Metropolitan Police Act 1829

2. There are a number of collections of parish truncheons or staffs in museums and private hands. Many can be seen at the Police Staff College and the Castle Museum at York. "The Policeman's Lot" by M.A.Mitton (1986), deals with truncheons and other items of police equipment. With a bit of diligent research it just might be possible to track down a parish staff actually carried by an ancestor who was a parish constable.

3. Henry Feilding, the novelist and playwright, was a Magistrate at the Bow Street office from 1748 until 1754. Thereafter his half brother John, later Sir John, Fielding took over the office until 1780. Both brothers experimented with different areas of police reform and both published works on the subject.

4. See "Paper Pursuit" by L.A.Waters in Police History Society Journal No 1 (1986) p30

5. These additional Public Offices were;
    Great Marlborough Street
    Queens Square
    Hatton Garden
    Worship Street
    Lambeth Street
    High Street Shadwell
    Union Street Southwark

6. For example the 'Newmarket Felons'

7. See Gerald Howson "Thief Taker General" (Hutchinson 1970) now in print under the title "It Takes A Thief" (Cresset 1987)

8. See David Ascoli "The Queen's Peace" (Hamish Hamilton 1979) pp 78 - 100, T.A.Critchley "A History Of Police In England And Wales" (Constable 1978 Edn) pp 51 - 57.

9. These could be indexed under "lighting", "paving" or "watching".

10. A classic example is to be found in the Cambridgeshire County Record Office in the form of the "Day Book Of The Cottenham Police".

11. There were 178 Boroughs covered by the Act of 1835. The Watch Committee was to consist of the Mayor plus not more than one third of the town council.

12. H.O. 73.2 - H.O. 73.9

13. See F.C.Mather "Public Order In The Age Of The Chartists" (1959) p 128

14. For a good account of the effect of the Act see David Foster "The Rural Constabulary Act 1839" (Standing Conference For Local History 1982)

15. PP Vol XXXVI (Police) Session 1852-3

16. Op. cit. pp 101 - 295

17. No doubt the poor rates of pay for constables also played a part. At one point in the 1830s the annual rate of wastage in the Metropolitan Police was 33% of the strength.

18. In some County Record Offices these are known as the "Session Rolls".

19. 1 Geo 4 c.37 ss 1 and 2 and Special Constables Act 1831

20. For an account of railway police history see J.R.Whitbread "The Railway Policeman" (Harrap 1961). Another specialised non Home Office Police is covered in Glyn Hardwicke's "Keepers Of The Door" (Peel Press 1979) (Port Of London Authority Police)

Police History Society, Notes For Family Historians

Appendix A
Current U.K. Police Forces and their Headquarters' Addresses.

Figures refer to the map following.

1. Avon and Somerset Constabulary
   P.O.Box 1888, Bristol BS99 7BH

2. Bedfordshire Police,
   Woburn Road, Kempston, Bedford MK43 9AX

3. Cambridgeshire Constabulary,
   Hinchingbrooke Park, Huntingdon, Cambridgeshire PE18 8NP

4. Cheshire Constabulary,
   Castle Esplanade, Chester CH1 2PP

5. City of London Police,
   26 Old Jewry, London EC2R 8DJ

6. Cleveland Constabulary,
   PO Box 70, Dunning Road, Middlesborough,   Cleveland TS1 2AR

7. Cumbria Constabulary,
   Carleton Hall, Penrith, Cumbria CA10 2AU

8. Derbyshire Constabulary,
   Butterley Hall, Ripley, Derby DE5 3RS

9. Devon and Cornwall Constabulary,
   Middlemoor, Exeter EX2 7HQ

10. Dorset Police,
    Winfrith, Dorchester, Dorset DT2 8DZ

11. Durham Constabulary
    Aykley Heads, Durham DH1 5TT

12. Dyfed Powys Police
    Friar's Park, Carmarthen SA31 3AW

13. Essex Police
    P.O.Box 2 Springfield, Chelmsford, Essex CM2 6DA

14. Gloucestershire Constabulary
    Holland House, Lansdown Road, Cheltenham, Gloucestershire GL51 6QH

15. Greater Manchester Police
    P.O.Box 22, Chester House, Boyer Street, Manchester M16 0RE

16. Gwent Constabulary
    Croesyceilliog, Cwmbram, Gwent NP44 2XJ

17. Hampshire Constabulary
    West Hill, Winchester, Hants SO22 5DB

18. Hertfordshire Constabulary
    Stanborough Road, Welwyn Garden City, Herts, AL8 6XF

19. Humberside Police
    Queens Gardens, Kingston upon Hull, Humberside, HU1 3DJ

20. Kent Constabulary
    Sutton Road, Maidstone, Kent, ME15 9BZ

21. Lancashire Constabulary
    Hutton, Nr. Preston, Lancs, PR4 5SB

22. Leicestershire Constabulary
    "Ashleigh", 420 London Road, Leicester LE2 2PT

23. Lincolnshire Police
    P.O. Box 999, Lincoln, LN5 7PH

24. Merseyside
    P.O. Box 59, Liverpool L691JD

25. Metropolitan Police
    New Scotland Yard, Broadway, London SW1H 0BG

26. Norfolk Constabulary
    Martineau Lane, Norwich, Norfolk NR1 2DJ

27. Northamptonshire Police
    Wootton Hall, Northampton, NN4 0JQ

28. Northumbria Police
    Ponteland, Newcastle upon Tyne, NE20 0BL

29. North Wales Police
    Colwyn Bay

30. North Yorkshire Police
    Newby Wiske Hall, Northallerton, Yorkshire, DL7 9HA

31. Nottinghamshire Constabulary
    Sherwood Lodge, Arnold, Nottingham NG5 8PP

32. South Wales Constabulary
    Bridgend, Glamorgan, South Wales

33. South Yorkshire Police
    Sheffield S3 8LY

34. Staffordshire Police
    Cannock Road, Stafford, ST17 0QG

35. Suffolk Constabulary
    Martlesham Heath, Ipswich, IP5 7QS

36. Surrey Constabulary
    Mount Browne, Sandy Lane, Guildford, Surrey GU3 1HG

37. Sussex Police
    Malling House, Lewes, Sussex BN7 2DZ

38. Thames Valley Police
    Kidlington, Oxford, OX5 2NX

39. Warwickshire Constabulary
    P.O. Box 4, Leek Wootton, Warwick, CV35 7QB

40. West Mercia Constabulary
    Hindlip Hall, Hindlip, Worcester, WR3 8SP

41. West Midlands Police
    P.O. Box 52, Lloyd House, Colmore Circus Queensway, Birmingham B4 6NQ

42. West Yorkshire Metropolitan Police
    P.O. Box 9, Wakefield, West Yorkshire, WF1 3QP.

43. Wiltshire Constabulary
    London Road, Devizes, Wiltshire, SN10 2DN

Ministry of Defence Police
Empress State Building, Lillie Road, London SW6 1TR

British Transport Police
P.O. Box 260, London WC1H 9SJ

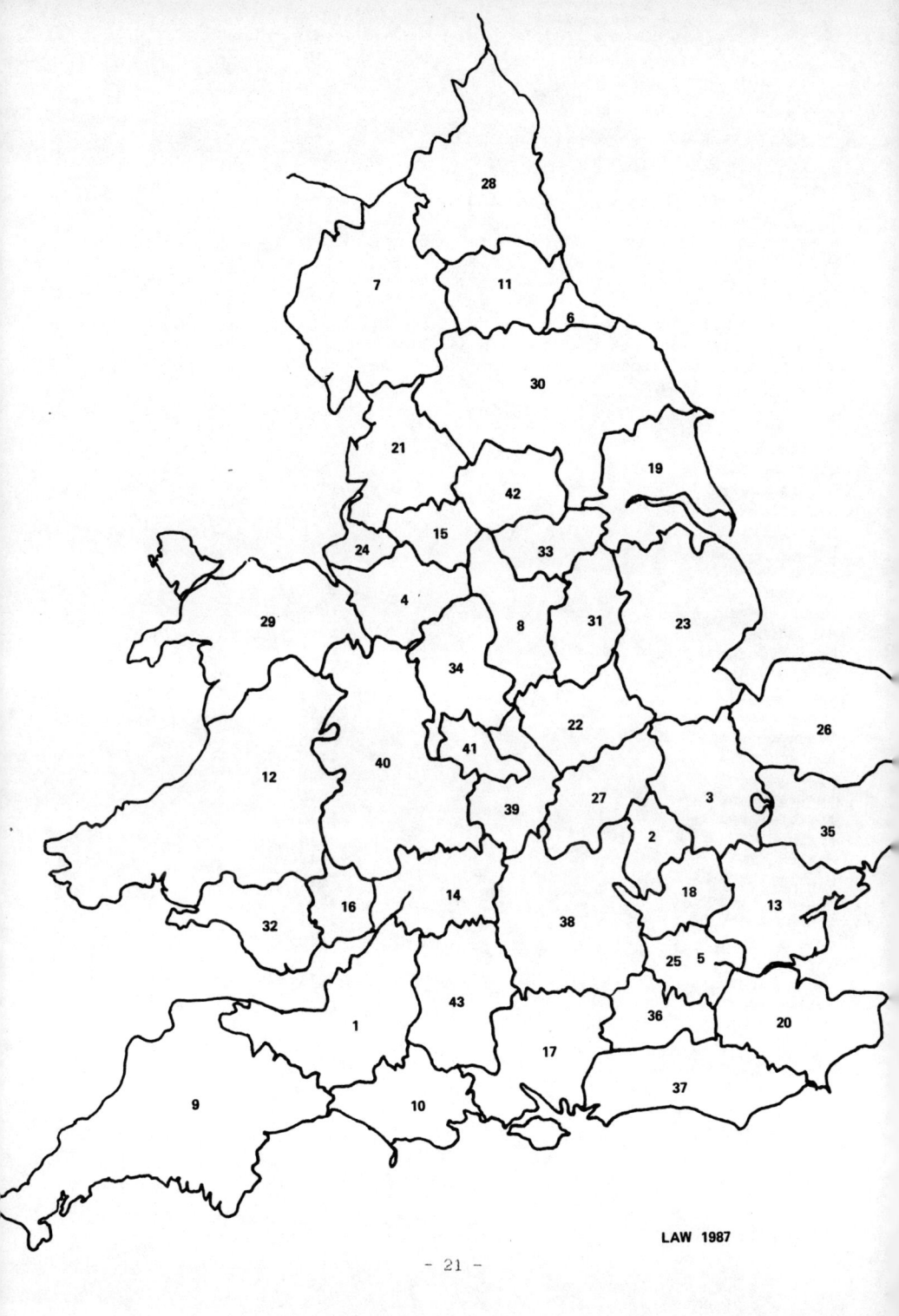

Police History Society, Notes For Family Historians

Appendix B.

County Police Forces And Dates Of Formation

Given below are approximate dates for the adoption of the 1839 County Police Act in different Counties. Those places not shown did not adopt this Act and those Forces were formed under the County and Borough Police Act of 1856.

Bedfordshire	1840
Cambridgeshire	1851
Cardiganshire	1844
Cumberland	1840
Denbighshire	1840
Durham	1839
Essex	1839
Glamorgan	1841
Gloucestershire	1839
Hampshire	1839
Herefordshire	1841
Hertfordshire	1841
Isle of Ely	1841
Lancashire	1839
Leicestershire	1839
Montgomeryshire	1840
Norfolk	1840
Northamptonshire	1840
Nottinghamshire	1840
Rutland	1848
Shropshire	1840
Staffordshire	1840
Suffolk (East)	1840
Surrey	1851
Sussex (East)	1840
Warwickshire	1840
Westmorland	1844
Wiltshire	1839
Worcestershire	1839

Appendix C

List Of Known Police Museums.

Forces with a permanent museum display of some sort, generally speaking not open to the public other than by special arrangement. If you wish to visit contact the force concerned to establish visiting arrangements

Bedfordshire
Cambridgeshire
City of London
Derbyshire
Devon and Cornwall
Gloucestershire
Gwent
Kent
Lancashire
Lincolnshire
Greater Manchester
Merseyside
Metropolitan Police
Northamptonshire
Royal Ulster Constabulary
South Wales
Suffolk
Sussex
Thames Valley
West Mercia
West Midlands
West Yorkshire

Forces with collections in store or with museums planned
Avon and Somerset
Cleveland
Dorset
Humberside
Leicestershire
Norfolk
Northumbria
Surrey
Warwickshire

There is also a combined N. Yorkshire Police and Prison Museum at St Mary Gate, Ripon.

APPENDIX D

THE POLICE AND CONSTABULARY ALMANAC

The Police and Constabulary Almanac is a unique reference work of great value to both police and the family historians. The Almanac has been produced annually in an unbroken series since 1858. At least the earliest surviving issue dates from that year but nothing in that volume actually indicates that it was a new venture. A commencement date of 1858 does however make sense as some counties had only established their new forces the previous year under the County and Borough Police Act of 1856. It is interesting to note that the current publishers of this invaluable work only claim a pedigree dating from 1861. (That other famous Almanac, Whittaker's, started 10 years later in 1868)

The Almanac was first published by Thomas Sowler and Sons, St Ann's Square, Manchester, printers and proprietors of the Conservative "Manchester Courier" newspaper. The compiler during the first two years was stated to be one Edwin Sheppard of Blackburn. (Any relation to Captain T.W.Sheppard, Chief Constable of Lancashire, or was he simply an employee of the publishers? In either case he does not seem to have been the author of any other works)

Originally the Almanac contained details of all County and Borough forces, their Divisions and senior officers down to Superintendent level. A calendar section gave important dates and the times of sun and moon rise and set. Other sections included Cabinet Ministers, Her Majesty's Inspectors of Constabulary, Judges, Reformatory Schools and Post Office arrangements, together with a few advertisements and a survey of important new legislation from the previous parliamentary session. For each police division details were given of population, acreage, property valuation and police strength. The 1858 almanac ran to 56 pages plus advertisements.

In its 1859 edition some obvious omissions were corrected, again suggesting that 1858 was the first year of publication. Irish policing arrangements and details of the Editor of the Police Gazette were added.

Gradually additional valuable information was added to succeeding annual volumes. The main additions up to 1920 are summarised below

Details	From	To
Scottish Procurators fiscal	1862	
Governors and Chaplains of Convict Prisons and County and Borough Gaols	1862	
Certified Industrial Schools	1864	
R.S.P.C.A. Brief details only	1864	1904
Full details of officers	1905	
Railway Police Forces and senior officers	1865	

Police Mutual Assurance Co details & Committee	1868	
Alphabetical list of Chief Constables in name order (including year of appointment)	1869 1901 1910	1878 (1)
Alphabetical list of Superintendents	1869 1901	1878 (1)
Police Orphan Home location and officers	1870	
Inspector of Meat at Spittalfield	1870	
Isle of Man Police	1875	
Chairmen of Police Committees	1875	
Chairmen of Quarter Sessions, Recorders in towns, Clerks of Peace	1876	
Convict Prison Department officials	1877	
List of Chief Constables and Superintendents arranged in alphabetical order based upon place stationed.	1879	
Refuges for female convicts	1885	
Truant Industrial Schools	1886	
Coroners	1889	
Legalised police cells in Scotland	1889	
Main County Council officials	1890	
Military Prisons	1891	
Police Telegraph Code	1891	(2)
Unions and their officers	1892	
County, United County and Borough Assylums, including details of Medical Superintendents and clerks	1894	
General facts concerning the police nationally, including No of officers and cost of service.	1890	
Reformatory for Fallen and Friendless Females	1894	
Home, War and Admiralty Department permanent senior officials	1893	

Assylums in Scotland	1895
Lunatic Hospitals	1895
Supreme Court of Judicature	1876
Early shopping days in main towns	1898
Lighting up times (initially entitled 'Cyclists Lighting Table')	1901
Qualifications required by different forces for candidates.	1903
Motor number index and list of persons authorised to grant motor licences	1906
Police Information Guide which gives details of the numbers of different types of premises and dealers in the force.	1906
N.S.P.C.C. officials	1908
Institutions for epileptics and persons suffering from nervous disorder	1912
Manchester Dock Police	1915
Officials of County Chief Constables Club Chief Constables Assn of Boroughs and Cities and Chief Constables Club (Scotland)	1912
Table of City and Borough Police with Corporation Fire Brigades	1915
Police Court and Prison Gate Missionaries	1917
Retreats under Licence	1917
Naval and Military Hospitals	1920

The information supplied concerning the officers of police forces was progressively widened over the period reviewed and from about 1880 names of Inspectors and even some Sergeants started to appear. In relation to other topics covered the names of appropriate officials were normally shown.

From 1920 there were other minor changes, taking into account new legislation and gradually widening the scope of the information given. The most important revision took place in 1972. The book was enlarged by 40% and an excellent gazetteer of police stations was added together with a list of Crown Courts. In 1973 the detailed contents list which had been present at the front of the book since 1858 was replaced by a comprehensive index.

The question of the gazetteer section is interesting as it was obviously felt to be an important omission at an earlier stage. The original publishers, T. Sowler & Co, produced another interesting publication in 1884 entitled the "Index to Police Forces in England Scotland and Wales" compiled by Francis J. Kirchner of the Criminal Investigation Department at Great Scotland Yard. This work, originally running to 100 pages at a price of one shilling, is mainly an index and gazetteer intended to complement the Almanac. The work was intended to be less ephemeral than the Almanac and contains no personal details of any officers. [3]

From 1858 to 1920 the Almanac grew steadily to 244 pages. (Today it just tops 300 pages) The cost of the publication remained at 1 shilling and sixpence from 1858 to 1909. Price rises then took place as follows; 1909...1/8d.   1917...1/9d.   1918...2/-.   1919...2/9d.   1920...3/6d

So far as advertisements are concerned we are sadly deprived of most of those included in the Almanacs as they were either printed on the endpapers or loose inserts, both of which have not survived later binding of the few remaining copies. Of the few early items which have survived there were three private detective agencies who were advertising via the Almanac at a relatively early stage. These were Finney & Co of Woburn Chambers, 22 Henrietta Street Covent Garden (1871), Worledge's Confidential Agency of 16 Moreton Place, Charlewood Street, Pimlico (1879) and The British and Foreign Private Inquiry Office (Mr N. Druscovich) 64 South Lambeth Road (1882). (Worledge advertised as his claim to fame that he was the nephew of the late Mr Field of the Metropolitan Detective Police!) Other interesting early advertisements were for Parker, Field and Sons, police armourers of 233 High Holborn (1858), "The Police Guardian", "Police and Fire" and "The Fireman" periodicals (all in 1883), Coventry Constabulary Cycle Company (1895) and The Cab Drivers Benevolent Institution (1880).[4] There were many other advertisements for uniform manufacturers and various ubiquitous patent medicines.

The publishers of the Almanac changed their company name to "The Manchester Courier Ltd." in 1906. The Manchester Courier ceased production in January 1916 and the 1919 edition shows that the Almanac had been taken over by R. Hazell of Fulwood House, High Holborn, London WC1. [5]

The Company still produce this valuable reference work from Henley on Thames and the Editor, since 1970 is Mr C.G.A. Parker. [6].

The Police and Constabulary Almanac is a little known source of historical information, partly because of its ephemeral nature and narrow specialist subject matter and partly because of the scarcity of survivals. The publishers lost their entire stock and records during the 1939 - 1945 war. Because of this they kept no records for many years afterwards and when the current owner took over in 1970 from Mr Alfred W. Hampstead the only stock consisted of one copy of the 1970 Almanac.

A complete run of the Police and Constabulary Almanac [7] can be found at the Police Staff College Library, Bramshill House, Near Hartley Wintney, Hampshire. Scolars wishing to consult the work are advised to write to the Librarian to seek permission to visit. Obviously in view of the value of these works they cannot be released on loan.

Outside the Police Staff College survivals are few. Some police museums have odd copies of the Almanac and the British Library have a single survival from 1861 plus copies from 1962. Regretably no other holdings in major libraries are listed in the British Union Catalogue of periodicals. (The author has access to copies in Cambridgeshire for the period 1874 - 1889 and can assist with some searches but it is stressed that this source is not applicable to Constables and that the higher the rank of the officer the more likely he is to be listed.)

Police History Society, Notes For Family Historians

NOTES — APPENDIX D

1. There is a significant gap here between the years 1878 and 1901 when these useful tables were excluded

2. The Police Telegraph Code is worthy of comment. The appearance of the code followed the reduction on 1st October 1885 of public telegraph fees to 6d for up to 12 words plus ½d for each subsequent word. The code was intended to add a degree of privacy and authenticity to telegraphs between forces and to keep down the cost of such messages. The code consists of some 314 words and numbers, each of which represents a well used police phrase. A message format listing the order in which information was to be coded and a numbered list of police stations completed the system. The words used were in English but were the sort of words which were unlikely to otherwise appear in a police circulation. Interestingly this was not the only police telegraph code in existance. A more complex code using some 2155 latin words had been devised in 1885 by Detective Chief Superintendent Frederick Williamson of the Metropolitan Police. Williamson's code appears to have been intended more for communication between police and government departments and British Ambassadors and Consuls abroad. The Almanac does not give any acknowledgement to any inventor of the code used. The code must have been used successfully as it was retained in the Almanac from 1891 to 1946. During that period the Almanac wat re-named "The Police and Constabulary Almanac, Official Register and Telegraph Code". The use of telegraph codes was common place in many industries, trades and professions during this period. The B.L. Subject Catalogue for the period 1881 - 1900 lists 152 different books of telegraph codes which had found their way into the British Library and there must have been many more which escaped collection.

3. F.J.Kirchner's Index appears to have been published in the following years; 1884, 1886, 1893, 1908 and 1931. The title was changed in 1893 to the "Index to the Police Forces of the British Empire and the United States of America and Foreign Countries". No names of officials are shown in any editions. The last two editions of the Index were published by the Police Review and the final edition was prepared by Divisional Detective Inspector A.H.K.Kirchner of New Scotland Yard, the son of the original Kirchner, then deceased, who had retiring from the Metropolitan Police as a Superintendent in 1910. These works are in the British Library and issues of 1884, 1908 and 1931 are in the Cambridge University Library.

4. Each and every one of these items would be worthy of further research. Particularly the history of private detective agencies appears to be virgin territory for the amateur or local historian

5. R.Hazell and Co appear to have operated from the following addresses;

1945	Rhodes Minnis, Elham, Canterbury, Kent.
1960	Alpha House, 152 Rye Lane, London SE15.
1971	3 & 4 Clements Inn, London WC2A 2DU.
1973	326 St John Street, London EC1V 4QD.
1976	117 Hatfield Road, St Albans.
1980	PO Box 39 Henley on Thames, Oxfordshire.

6. R.Hazell and Co now also produce (since 1985) an annual law directory entitled "Hazell's Guide". The company is also linked with another publisher in producing the quarterly "Police Studies" journal and the biennial "International Security Directory". They also, from time to time, publish books on police related topics. Hazell and Co are also now associated with another company which produces the monthly periodical "Security Gazette"

7. Save 1911 Edition which lacks pp 128-211.

APPENDIX E

NOTES ON POLICE PERIODICALS

IN THE BRITISH LIBRARY & ELSEWHERE

(Up to 1920)

The following "police" periodicals appear in the index to the British Library Newspaper Library at Colindale Avenue, London NW9 5HE, the B.L. Catalogue and the British Union Catalogue of Periodicals.

Bulls Eye   August 1920 - December 1922

A political fortnightly publication by the British Union of Police and Prison Officers concerning their fight for better conditions and in the aftermath of the Police Strike of 1919. Very few names appear in this journal but it does contain interesting material in support of the Union. Copies are also in the University Library, Cambridge.

Cleave's Weekly Police Gazette 1835 and 1836

A comprehensive working class general newspaper. Although there is a heavy weighting of reports of cases from the police and other courts this is of little value to the family historian unless researching a particular crime. Copies also in the University Library, Cambridge.

The Fireman June 1877 -

Although originally intended for firemen there were strong efforts made to give this periodical a dual readership particularly as many borough police forces were also local fire brigades. For the most part however the periodical deals with appliances, equipment, techniques, incidents and news connected with the fire service. There is little biographical material but there is a good annual index.

Copies are also held in the University Library, Cambridge, Patent Office Library (1877-1917), National Library of Scotland (Vol 17-), Ratcliffe Science Library, Oxford (Vol 11-).

The Hue and Cry and Police Gazette

See Police Gazette

On and Off Duty September 1883 - Circa 1920

This monthly periodical was the official voice of the Christian Policemen's Association, which had been founded in February 1883. The periodical later also appears to have some connection with the Police Missionary Union. On

And Off Duty was first published from 186 Aldersgate Street, London, later
from 1a Adelphi Terrace, Strand, London W.C. This monthly periodical
contains news and miscellany connected with the police with a christian
slant. The periodical does contain some detailed obituaries and details of
brave deeds by police as well as small pieces of news headed "Flashes From
The Forces" and there is also a rather skimpy annual index.
This periodical is in the main British Library and not at the National
Newspaper Library at Colindale, copies also exist in the University Library,
Cambridge.

Peoples Police Gazette 1841

Very similar to Cleave's Weekly Police Gazette above.

Police and Fire 1880 - 1883 ?

Issues exist at Colindale for 1.6.1880 (No 1), 28.5.1881 and 21.7.1883
Published by Jenkyn Ingram, the original Editor of The Fireman, of 7
Booksellers Row, the Strand, London W.C. This periodical contains news and
information on public safety relating to the police and fire services, both
metropolitan and provincial.

Police and Prison Officers Journal 1914 - 1915

First clandestine Journal of the Police and Prison Officers Union. See notes
above re Bulls Eye. Copies are in the British Library not at Colindale.

Police and Prison Officers Magazine 1918 - 1919

Continuation of the above. Again copies are not at Colindale but are in the
main B.L.

Police and Public 1889

Survivals at Colindale are dated 6.7.1889- 14.9.1889. This is a general
newspaper with a slant towards crime reporting and real life tragedies. It
was continued from 21.9.1889 to 21.12.1889 under the title of The
Illustrated Weekly News before being discontinued. Although essentially not
a police periodical this serial is worth a mention as it does carry some
material on the Whitechapel (Jack the Ripper) murders.

Police Bits Illustrated 1896

Issues exist for 10th July 1896 - 14th August 1896. The first issue is
suprisingly a sporting periodical. Later issues do however relate to
sensational crimes and tragedies. Published by Frank Shaw of Caxton House,
11, Gough Square, Fleet Street.

The Police Chronicle

See the Police Service Advertiser

The Police Chronicle and Constabulary World

See the Police Service Advertiser

The Police Gazette 1828 -

The Gazette was originally conceived by Sir John Fielding following the successes in crime detection achieved by public advertising by both himself and previously by his half brother Henry Fielding. Sir John Fielding's circulations to Magistrates and Mayors were known as the "Quarterly Pursuit" and "Weekly Pursuit". His successor at Bow Street, Sir Sampson Wright, updated these efforts and produced a weekly periodical entitled "Public Hue and Cry" from 1786. The title changed again in 1795 to "The Hue and Cry and Police Gazette" and again in 1828 the name was changed to the present title "The Police Gazette". It is still in print and has been published by the Metropolitan Police since 1883.

The Gazette contains details of major and minor unsolved crime, nationwide. Details are given of persons arrested who may be wanted elsewhere as well as descriptions of wanted and escaped persons. There are also details and descriptions of deserters and persons absent without leave from the armed forces, including descriptions and dates and places of birth. With each item there is also given the name and place of office of a senior officer as a contact. This valuable and largely untapped source contains millions of names but is not indexed.

The British Library holds copies of the Gazette from 1801, 1802, 1815, 1818 - 1834, 1858, 1877 - . A detailed finding list of other copies of the Gazette in major libraries, County Record Offices and police museums accompanies an article on the Gazette entitled "Paper Pursuit" in Journal No 1 of the Police History Society.

The Police Guardian and Advertiser

See Police Service Advertiser.

Police News Miscellany 1877

Survivals are dated 24.3.1877 - 2.6.1877. This is a sensational journal of fact and fiction.

The Police Recorder 1838

Survivals exist from 23.9.1838 - 30.12.1838.

A general newspaper consisting mainly of detailed weekly reports of crime from the various London Police Courts. The editor claimed initially, with some justification, that this was the largest folio newspaper ever produced. The publisher was Richard Egan Lee, 20 Old Boswell Court, Temple Bar, London. There is an interesting series of articles in the first six issues entitled "Recollections of a Bow Street Runner". With effect from 1839 the paper continued as The Recorder, a London weekly newspaper.

The Police Reporter and Criminal Record 1854

Issues survive for 11.2.1854 and 18.2.1854

This newspaper contains reports from criminal courts, mainly in London, and reports of disasters and national and international events. It also contains historical articles on the lives of the most famous criminals. Published by Appleyard and Hetling, 86 Farringdon Street, London

The Police Review and Parade Gossip 1893 –

This periodical commenced on 2.1.1893. From 29.6.1934 it was continued to date as The Police Review. There is a complete run at The Newspaper Library at Colindale. Copies from 1893 - 1919 can also be found in the Manchester Public Library. Complete runs of the Review are also to be found at the Police Staff College and at the office of the Review at 14 St Cross Street, London EC1N 8FE.

A very useful periodical produced for police officers and their families. The Review carried (and still carries) items on conditions of service, police methods, news relating to the service and serving officers, including biographical material on top officers and some police celebrities. There is also a valuable annual index.

Of all the police periodicals published this is probably the most valuable to the researcher for the period it covers. The Review also currently regularly features articles on historical material, including four pages per quarter carrying material from the Police History Society.

The Police Service Advertiser 1866 – 1959 (under various titles)

First issued Saturday Feb 3rd 1866.

Originally this serial was sub titled "A Journal for the Police and Constabulary Forces of G.B. and the Colonies. Weekly on Saturdays." This periodical championed a number of improvements in conditions of service for police officers. The periodical contains news items connected with the police and crime, including obituaries. In its early days the paper contained a number of other features of ordinary newspapers such as market prices, parliamentary report and even gardening tips. Annual Reports from Her Majesty's Inspectors of Constabularies and from Chief Constables also feature. There was a lively "letters column" but most of the correspondents used "noms de plume". This would appear to have been wise as one of the more outspoken columnists, "La Verdad", lost his post as a Constable in Hampshire following some very pointed criticism of his Chief Constable.

Initially the Editor obviously saw that the Advertiser might take on something of the role of the Police Gazette in carrying engravings of photographs of "missing friends, absconded defaulters and wanted criminals". Although a few such engravings were carried and some "wanted person advertisements" appeared this role never really developed as the Editor had hoped.

The Advertiser was closely involved in establishing and promoting the Police Mutual Assurance Association in 1866 and became its unofficial organ. As such for many years the paper carried notices of the deaths of members of the Association and subscription lists of the stations subscribing towards the death benefit for the deceased's family. This is therefore a useful source of information if an officer died in service (if he was a subscriber to the Police Mutual Assurance Association).

As it progressed the Advertiser carried recruiting advertisements for police officers, details of new law, presentations to serving officers, police murders, serious crime and announcements of births, marriages and deaths.

The original publisher was Thomas Fell Molyneux of 51A Victoria Street, Windsor, Berks (later known as the Royal Windsor Press).

Numerous police welfare issues were raised during the life of this periodical. On some occasions criticism of conditions of service even waxed poetical as in the following item from 1883 following a spate of untimely resignations;

"Oh Mister Chief Hinspector,
'Ere's my trunchin and my lamp,
and 'ere's the blessed bracelits
rayther rusty with the damp.
It's rained all night like cats and dogs,
Hi'm like a drown'd bald pup -
This job's a deal to good for me,
And so I chucks it up.

"I'll have no more policemanin'
It don't suit me, not quite;
I'd sooner be a soldierin'
a seein' fellows fight.
Taint nice bein' rained on
hours an' hours,
(and don't it rain a sup)-
This job's a deal to good for me
and so I chucks it up.

"To walk about the nasty streets
all through the nasty night
in nasty boots as pinch your feet,
and yet aint watertight
When hev'ry blessed kitchen's shut
in hev'ry blessed street;
And not a blessed cook about
to tip us some cold meat.

"Of all the cloathes I've ever 'ad,
the p'liceman's is the worst,
I aint bin dry for weeks and weeks,
exceptin' in my thirst;
but no one offers me a glass
O nothin', not a drup
The're all in bed when my jobs on
and so I chucks it up.

"No more policemanin for me,
at two and ten a night,
I think my life's worth more than that,
a precious, precious, sight "
and so he empties to the dregs
His life's sad bitter cup
His job's a deal too good for him
and so he chucks it up.

The Advertiser became "The Police Guardian And Advertiser" with effect from 3rd January 1873. (Sub-titled "A newspaper devoted to the interests of the police and constabulary of the United Kingdon and Colonies. Journal of prison and jail intelligence; City, Borough and County Magistrate"). This title was still published by Molyneux

By February 1888 the Police Guardian and Advertiser was subtitled "A Journal Devoted to the Interests of the Police and Constabulary Forces in the United Kingdom and the Colonies. Fire Brigade Journal. Assylum Prison and Reformatory Gazette. Watch Committee, Sanitary Authority, Union and Local Government Advertiser." With effect from 16.6.1888 The Advertiser became The Police Chronicle as the Chronicle and the Guardian combined after the former purchased the latter. The Chronicle appears to have started at some unknown date prior to 16th June 1888 (numbered as No 87 old series and No 37 new series)The Publisher became Mr H. Vickers 317 The Strand and the Chronicle was printed in Leamington. The Chronicle continued as the official organ of the P.M.A.A.

The Chronicle became The Police Chronicle and Constabulary World from 16th November 1934 until it ceased production 11th December 1959. In its latter days it had become a small format magazine catering not just for police officers but also for their families.

Unfortunately this interesting periodical was never indexed. There is a run of the periodical at Colindale from 3rd February 1866 to 11th December 1959.

The Policemans Watch

One issue is recorded for 1898. This is not however any sort of periodical but a single page advertising sheet for watches for policemen !

The Policewoman

One registration front sheet is saved at Colindale. This is dated September 1915 and was published by John Kempster, 8 Red Lion Square, London WC.

The Policewoman's Review

Colindale has a run from May 1927 - December 1937. This very specialised periodical was published by The Womens Auxilliary Service, (Late Women Police Service) 68 Victoria Street London SW1. Chief Constables requiring female officers were advised by advertisement to contact the W.A.S. for details of suitable women already trained in policewomen' duties.

The P.W.s Review contains a wealth of detail on women in the service, including a number of photographs of the policewomen of the day, often the first appointees, in different forces.

Police History Society, Notes For Family Historians

APPENDIX F

NOTES ON THE FIRST REPORT OF THE CONSTABULARY COMMISSIONERS

The three Commissioners appointed in 1836 to inquire into the best means of establishing an efficient constabulary force in the counties of England and Wales were;
    Colonel Charles Rowan (Commissioner of the Metropolitan Police)
    Edwin Chadwick Esq and
    Charles Shaw Lefevre, country gentleman.

In their report published in 1839 the Commissioners recommended that the counties should be policed by a properly trained and equipped preventative police force on the lines of the Metropolitan Police, where the magistrates so wished. They envisaged a force which would be one quarter funded from central government and three quarters funded by local rates. All ranks would be liable to work to local magistrates, by whom they could be removed from office. The general management of the police would be under rules framed by the Commissioners. Such an outcome of the Commission could easily have been predicted. Colonel Rowan was in no small part responsible for the success of the Metropolitan Police. Chadwick was also committed to the idea, having earlier written a treatise on preventative policing. Lefevre appears to have played only a small part in the proceedings.

What appear to be the complete papers collected and used by the Commissioners are deposited in the Public Record Office at Kew under references H.O.73.2 to H.O.73.9. The first important point is that the 14 boxes of material (H.O.73.4 - 9 are each in two boxes) are not catalogued or indexed in any way.

The original material is however a rich source of detail for the police historian. H.O 73.2 - 3 contain general correspondence and some unique proposals and interesting figures. (28) It is the following boxes however which contain the most exciting and interesting material. The Commissioners sent out three different sets of printed questionnaires to Magistrates, members of watch committees, and Guardians under the Poor Laws. These original returns, in their hundreds, are to be found in the remaining boxes.

The 1839 Report paints a picture of complete lawlessness in the country with virtually no policing outside London and with bands of criminals displaced into the countryside in the face of an efficient and effective Metropolitan Police. The report faithfully reproduces material supplied in questionnaires which had been submitted to the Commissioners. What is not included in the report is any measure of the overall degree of disatisfaction with the old parochial system in the country. There were in fact many returns testifying to a somewhat less universally lawless countryside than the Commissioners would have had us believe. The family or local historian interested in the effectiveness of pre 1839 policing in a certain locality can learn a great deal from these questionnaires of the past, once the right returns have been located.

Set out below is the questionnaire sent out to magistrates. The other two questionnaires follow broadly similar lines. This gives something of an insight into the level of detailed material to be found at Kew.

****

Where any Magistrate of the Petty Sessions may be desirous of answering any questions individually, those answers should each be distinguished by the initials of the Magistrate making them.

1. What is the extent and supposed population of the division for which you act ?

2. What number of acting Magistrates reside generally within your division ?

3. State, as nearly as you can, the number of felonies and misdemeanours committed during the last twelve months within your division ?

4. What proportion of the offenders has been apprehended ?

5. Do the constables apprehend offenders without being specifically applied to for that purpose ?

6. To what causes do you ascribe the failure to bring the offenders to justice; and have such failures been ascribable in any cases to the inefficiency of the constables ?

7. Are there any, and what peculiar facilities or inducements to the commission of crime within your division ?

8. By what means, as you conceive, may they be removed ?

9. In case of depredation in your division, is escape with the property easy; and is such property easily disposed of ?

10. Is there reason to believe that the depredations committed within your division have been committed by persons who do not reside in it; if so, from what place or direction are they supposed to come ?

11. Are there within your division any lodging houses for trampers, vagrants or mendicants or any peculiar inducements to vagrancy or mendicancy ?

12. Are these lodging houses frequently inspected; and by what officers?

13. Are offenders frequently apprehended there ?

14. Are there within your division any persons who have no visible or known means of obtaining their livelihood honestly, and who are believed to live by habitual depredation, or by illegal means ? Will you state the number and supposed habits of such persons ?

15. Are the beer shops or public - houses within your division the subject of complaint; and are they, in point of fact, ill conducted ?

16. Since the year 1829 have there been any riots or tumults within your division ? If any, describe them and their supposed objects.

17. Since the year 1829 have there been any fires within your division ? If so, specify their nature, and whether they were suspected to have been wilfully caused; and what were the effects so far as relates to the loss of life or property ?

18. Was any efficient assistance rendered by the constables in arresting the progress of the fires, or in apprehending the offenders or suspected persons ?

19. Since the same period have there been any malicious injuries committed on cattle or other property; and if so, what number ?

20. Is there reason to believe that offences of any description within your division are much more frequent than any official information would give reason to suppose ?

21. What is the number of constables in your division, and how are they appointed ?

22. From what class of persons are they usually selected, and are they permitted to provide substitutes ?

23. What description of persons usually serve as substitutes ?

24. What is usually paid to them by the principal ?

25. Have the persons serving as substitutes any other emoluments or inducements to serve the office ?

26. Have constables or their substitutes a competent knowledge of the law with relation to the duties of their office ?

27. Are their connexions or interests such as might tempt them to connive at illegal practices, or cause them to be less active than they ought to be in the performance of their duty ?

28. Can you ascertain, by examining competent persons who have served the office of Constable, what is the annual cost on an average to the public, and the individual, of the services of a constable during the year ?

29. Does any nightly patrol appear to be requisite within your division?

30. Do the high roads in your division require patrolling ?

31. In case of the commission of any offence, are there any public means of promptly spreading information or of pursuing the offender ? Describe the means, and specify the extent of district over which such information can be carried; in what time, and at what cost ?

32. In the case of the occurance of any riots or tumults, what means are available for their suppression, and for the apprehension of the offenders; and do you find any difficulty in securing the prompt attendance of a sufficient number of persons to act efficiently as special constables for the protection of your division ?

33. In case of need, are there and what means of co-operation between your division and other divisions in the same or different counties ?

34. Are there within your division any, and what class of persons such as army pensioners or others, who may be relied upon for trustworthy service as special constables ?

35. Is any difficulty or delay experienced in the service of warrants, or the execution of processes, or in the performance of their duties, civil and penal, by constables as at present appointed within your division ? If so, specify the difficulties and their consequences ?

36. Do any delays or obstructions arise from constables being restricted from acting beyond their immediate district ?

37. Are there within your division any, and what numbers of officers paid to keep the peace or give their whole time to the execution of their duties as constables ? If so, state what is the whole expence of maintaining them, including their salaries and equipments; the authority under which they are appointed, and the fund out of which they are paid.

38. On the apprehension of any offender, to what distance is it requisite to take him to a magistrate ?

39. In case a prisoner is remanded for further examination, in what place and manner is he secured; and to what distance is it necessary to send him to a place of legal confinement ?

40. In case he is committed for trial, what is the distance of the prison to which he must be sent; and what is the expense of his conveyance thither, including maintenance ?

41. Is any, and what part of the procedure before trial, the subject of complaint on account of trouble, delay, and expense ? If so, specify their effect in inducing persons to withhold information or otherwise.

42. Supposing it desirable to appoint paid constables to give their whole time to the performance of their duties, what other useful functions might be assigned to them ?

43. How many paid constables do you consider would be requisite in your division ?

44. Are there any voluntary associations for the protection of property or the prosecution of offenders within your division ? If so, describe them, and state their effects in preventing crime.

45. Is there within your division any voluntary association for the supression of vagrancy or mendicity ? If so, state its effects.

46. What proportion of the expences now incurred by the public in the apprehension and prosecution of offenders do you conceive might be saved by the establishment of a more efficient preventive force ?

47. Do any and what additional means appear to you to be desirable in your division for increasing the actual security, and the sense of security to persons and property ?

48. Have you any other information to give or suggestions to offer in furtherance of the objects of this commission ?

Signatures of the magistrates who make the answers ......

****

Police History Society, Notes For Family Historians

APPENDIX G

PUBLIC RECORD OFFICE

INFORMATION LEAFLET NUMBER 53

METROPOLITAN POLICE RECORDS OF SERVICE

ORGANISATION

The Metropolitan Police Act 1829 defined the original Metropolitan Police District as an area of about seven miles radius from Charing Cross. Within the next year seventeen police divisions were set up and centred on the following areas:

A - Westminster; B - Chelsea; C - Mayfair and Soho; D - Marylebone; E - Holborn; F - Kensington; G - Kings Cross; H - Stepney; K - West Ham; L - Lambeth; M - Southwark; N - Islington; P - Peckham; R - Greenwich; S - Hampstead; T - Hammersmith and V - Wandsworth.

In 1865 three more divisions were created, W - Clapham; X - Willesden and Y - Holloway, and J Division (Bethnal Green) was added in 1886. Maps of the districts and their changing boundaries can be found under the reference MEPO 15.

The Bow Street Horse Patrol was incorporated into the force in 1835 and operated in the outlying Metropolitan divisions. The second Metropolitan Police Act 1839 converted the River Thames force into the Thames Division, absorbed the Bow Street Foot Patrol and extended the Metropolitan Police District to a fifteen mile radius.

The establishment of the Metropolitan Police also had responsibility for the police of the Royal Dockyards and military stations, Portsmouth, Chatham, Devonport, Pembroke and Woolwich, from 1860 until 1934; information about dockyard police prior to 1860 might be found in the civil pensions for artificers and labourers (ADM 23).

Attempts to incorporate the City of London police into the force were unsuccessful and it has always retained its independence (see Other Forces).

Each division was in charge of a superintendent, under whom were four inspectors and sixteen sergeants. The regulations demanded that recruits should be under thirty-five, well built, at least five feet seven in height, literate and of good character. The minimum age is usually considered to be twenty years but the certificates of service (MEPO 4/361-477) include recruits as young as eighteen; service before the age of twenty was not considered for pension purposes.

STAFF RECORDS

Metropolitan Police staff records have not survived in their entirety and there are no records at all for the period May 1857-November 1869.

Nearly all the staff records detail name, rank, warrant number, division and dates of appointment and removal. Information additional to this has been noted in the records listed below:

Numerical registers of warrant numbers 1-3147, September 1829-March 1830 (MEPO 4/31-32) give the officer's height and cause of removal from the force.

Alphabetical register, 1829-1836 (HO 65/26) gives dates of promotion or demotion.

Alphabetical registers of joiners, September 1830-April 1857; July 1878-1933 (MEPO 4/333-338). The earliest volumes give names and addresses of referees.

Attestation ledgers for warrant numbers 51491-146379, December 1869-May 1958 (MEPO 4/352-360) give signatures of the recruit and witness.

Certificate of service records for warrant numbers 74201-97500, January 1889-November 1909 (MEPO 4/361-477) give a description of recruit, date of birth, trade, marital status, residence, number of children, name and place of last employer, previous public service, surgeon's certificate, postings to divisions, dates of promotion or demotion and cause of removal.

Registers of leavers, March 1889-January 1947 (MEPO 4/339-351) give class of officer, number of certificate granted if not dismissed (1. Excellent, 2. Very Good, 3. Good, 4. Open, i.e. no comment), date certificate sent to division, number of documents an officer entitled to, according to regulations, and date documents sent to division. These last two details are phased out around 1913-1914 and the comments on an officer's conduct are no longer expressed numerically. The abbreviation R.P. stands for 'resignation permitted' and is replaced in October 1920 by R.R. 'required to resign'. The divisional abbreviation C.O. stands for 'Commissioner's Office'.

The only set of records held at the Public Record Office which give the age of the officer are the registers of certificates of service, 1889-1909; it seems that no earlier or later records of this type have survived.

An index of names of officers is now being made available at the Public Record Office section by section as it is compiled by the Metropolitan Police Office. This is largely drawn from the registers of joiners, 1829-1836. It is not a complete index of all officers who have served in the Metropolitan Police, and does not necessarily include all the information about an individual officer which is to be found in the staff records.

Women police patrols were appointed to the force in February 1919 but they were not sworn in as constables with powers of arrest until April 1923. Unfortunately their records of service do not seem to have survived although the index mentioned above includes a separate section for them; the index gives warrant numbers, divisional numbers and dates of services.

OTHER SOURCES

The following records might supplement information found in the staff records described above:

Returns of deaths whilst serving, 1829-1889 (MEPO 4/2) give the cause of death.

Before the Police Pensions Act 1890 pensions were granted on a discretionary basis. The Act provided a legal right to a pension after twenty-five years service, and a modified pension or gratuity if discharged medically unfit. Pensions and gratuities, 1829-1859, are mentioned in the early series of correspondence and papers (MEPO 5/1-90).

The Pensions Branch, Metropolitan Police, New Scotland Yard, Victoria Street, London SW1 are still in possession of records, arranged by date of discharge, dating back to 1853 and they are willing to answer written enquiries.

Police Orders (MEPO 7) contain notification of personnel matters arranged annually. They are closed for fifty years. Details of officers pensioned, promoted, dismissed and transferred have been indexed for some of these volumes and added to the class (MEPO 7/156-164). An alphabetical index of officers who joined between 1880 and 1889, compiled from the Police Orders of those years (MEPO 7/42-51), is available in the Reference Room. Each entry consists of surname with at least one forename, warrant date, date of joining and (where available) date of leaving.

Joining papers and particulars of service of certain distinguished officers have been preserved amongst the Special Series of correspondence and papers from the Commissioner's Office (MEPO 3/2883-2921). These personnel files are subject to closure for at least seventy-five years.

Incomplete divisional records for A, B, E, F, G, H, K, L, M, N, R and Y divisions are held by the Records Section at New Scotland Yard. Thames Division ledgers are held at Wapping Police Station Museum, 98 Wapping High Street, London EC1. The Records Section and the Museum are not open to individual members of the public but they will try to answer written enquiries.

Files on awards of the Kings Police Medal from its introduction in 1909 can be found under the honours and awards subject code in the list to registered papers of the Home Office (HO 45) and a list of awards, 1909-1912, is given in MEPO 2/1300.

OTHER FORCES

Police records of other forces are not public records. Those which survive are held either by the appropriate local record office or the force itself.

Correspondence relating to colonial police forces can be found in the papers of the Colonial Office but the records of the forces themselves, like those of local forces in this country, are not held here but might well have been deposited in the archives of the country to which they relate.

The City of London Police Records Office, 26 Old Jewry, London EC2R 8OJ possesses registers listing every member of the force since warrant numbers were introduced on 9 April 1832 together with personal files on 95% of officers who have served since that date.

Records for the railway police of the various railway companies do not appear to be amongst the railway staff records held at the Public Record Office, but information about the numbers and organisation of railway police circa 1900 can be found in RAIL 527/1036. The occasional references to 'Police Department' in the railway staff records relate to signalmen etc.

There is a separate PRO leaflet describing records of service of the Royal Irish Constabulary.

ADMINISTRATIVE RECORDS

Other departmental records relating to the Metropolitan and other police forces can be found in MEPO 2, MEPO 3, MEPO 5 and MEPO 7 and amongst the records of the Home Office.

© Crown Copyright, September 1985

Police History Society, Notes For Family Historians

SELECTED BIBLIOGRAPHY

David Ascoli, The Queens Peace (Hamish Hamilton 1979)

Dennis Brett, Librarian Police Staff College, The Police Of England And Wales, A Bibliography, 1829 - 1979 (Police Staff College 1979)

Douglas C. Browne, The Rise Of Scotland Yard (Harrap 1956)

The Constabulary Commissioners, First Report (H.M.S.O. 1836)

T.A.Critchley, A History Of Police In England And Wales (Constable 1978)

B.J.Davey, Lawless And Immoral, Policing A Country Town 1838 - 1857 (1984)

Percy Fitzgerald, Chronicles Of Bow Street Police Office (Chapman and Hall 1888)

David Foster, The Rural Constabulary Act 1839 (Standing Conference For Local History 1982)

H.Goddard, Memoirs Of A Bow Street Runner (Museum Press 1956)

Home Office and Central Office Of Information, Story Of Our Police, an educational package in two parts (H.M.S.O. 1976 and 1977) Some forces still have free copies of this very useful package.

W.L.Melville Lee, A History Of Police In England (Methuen 1901)

L.Radzinowicz, A History Of English Criminal Law (Stevens 1948-1968)

Howard Ripley, Police Forces Of Great Britain And Ireland - Their Amalgamations And Their Buttons (Hazell 1983) (Although obviously an item for collectors of buttons this useful work has a comprehensive list of forces and their amalgamations and changes of name)

The Select Committee On Police, First And Second Reports (H.M.S.O. 1853)

Ronald Seth, The Specials (Gollancz 1961)

P.T.Smith, Policing Victorian London (Greenwood 1985)

P.J.Stead, The Police Of Britain (Macmillan 1985)

Carolyn Steedman, Policing The Victorian Community (Routledge & Kegan Paul 1984)

J.R.Whitbread, The Railway Policeman (Harrap 1961)

THE POLICE HISTORY SOCIETY

The Police History Society is an educational charity set up to promote interest in the history of policing and associated topics.

The Society publishes an annual Journal and quarterly Newsletters which are free to members.

The Society runs an annual Conference and is engaged in a number of projects linked to the preservation of archives and re-publication of scarce source material.

Membership of the Society is open to any person or organisation. The Annual subscription at the time of writing (1987) is £5.00. The Journal is available to non members at £4.00 per annum including postage.

All enquiries concerning membership should be directed to the Membership Secretary;

        Martin Stallion
        18 Cornec Chase
        Leigh on Sea
        ESSEX
        SS9 5EW

THE OFFICIAL TRICYCLE.

Suitable for persons from 12 to 20 stone.

THE above TRICYCLE is strongly recommended to Police Officers, Firemen, &c., for business purposes. Any person with a little practice can travel with ease eight miles per hour. Prices from £16.

Illustrated Catalogue of Tricycles, Bicycles, and Sewing Machines, Post Free on application.

H. J. NORRIS,
TRICYCLE AND BICYCLE OFFICES,
HERTFORD STREET, COVENTRY.